Joyce Thornton

THEOLOGY

THERE'S ALGAE IN THE BAPTISMAL 'FOUNT'

THERE'S ALGAE IN THE BAPTISMAL 'FOUNT'

Daniel Zeluff

designed and illustrated by steve laughbaum

Abingdon

Nashville

There's Algae in the Baptismal 'Fount'

Copyright © 1978 by Abingdon

All rights in this book are reserved.
No part of the book may be reproduced in any manner whatsoever without written permission of the publisher except brief quotations embodied in critical articles or reviews. For information address Abingdon, Nashville, Tennessee.

Library of Congress Cataloging in Publication Data

ZELUFF, DANIEL, 1930-
  There's algae in the baptismal 'fount'.

  1. Clergy—Psychology. 2. Pastoral theology. I. Title.
BV660.2.Z44   253'.2   77-13192
ISBN 0-687-41630-2

Manufactured by the Parthenon Press at Nashville, Tennessee, United States of America

To
Edna Alsdurf

Contents

Preface 9

Syndromes

Roadrunner 15
Room Service 18
Dirty Guys Blew Up My Roadway
  of Life 23
Clean Blackboard 26
I Must Be a Prophet, Else Why
  Are They Stoning Me? 27
Beef Jerky 31
Court Jester 33
Ha, Ha, Ha—Jab, Jab 35
Cool Hand Luke 37
He Walks with Me and He
  Talks with Me 38
Street Urchin 39
With-It-ness 43
Hark, I Perceive Thou Art
  a Dirty Dog 44
Plaster of Paris 47
Damascus Turnpike 50
Joan of Arc 54
Et Tu, Brute 57

Confessions of an Ex–Holy Man   64

Rx – Maybe

Work Is Not Necessarily Moral—
  It's Just Doing 74
Pleasure Is Better than Pain? 81
The Narcissistic Cowboy versus
  the Holy Mob 91
The Relief of Being Average 102

Preface

For the past seven years I have been a counselor to the clergy. I have listened to the problems, gripes, and the gnashing of teeth of ordained ministers and their families. Many were Roman Catholic. Most were Protestant. They represented over seventeen denominations from thirty-eight states with a smattering from Canada and Britain and a few smaller countries thrown in for flavor.

Some were young, freshly ordained, ready to put the world right, out to slay dragons and reestablish an Americanized Davidic kingdom. Others had been at it for ten to twelve years and were burned out, disillusioned, and ready to pack it in. A number were in their sixties, approaching retirement with no home to live in, no spare funds, wondering if the system they had served was, after all, all that trustworthy. In the last few years, many have been women discovering that they had to elbow their way into an almost totally male-dominated arena.

Many had doctorates. Most did not. A few of the most perceptive and well-educated had only high-school diplomas. All were interesting.

In these group and individual contacts with clergy, I was struck by two recurring themes. First, I noticed that most participants suffered from low self-esteem. They really did not like themselves very much. This has been validated in part by the low "K" factor in their Minnesota Multiphasic Personality Inventory scores.[1]

Second, there was a desire to avoid deep and lasting relationships. Avoidance of quick intimacy is of course expected in any seminar setting, and it is a healthy attitude. But, as the participants began to relax and relate, I learned that any intimacy was unique, and frightening. They had rarely, if ever, experienced this before.

As they began to talk of their style of ministry and their past experiences with

---

[1] *An MMPI Handbook*, W. Grant Dahlstrom and George Schlager Welsh, The University of Minnesota Press, Minneapolis, 1965.

people, a pattern of frequent but shallow relationship was revealed. Many complained of severe loneliness, all the while conscious of the protective devices that they were using to insulate themselves from more profound relationships. "My wife is the only one I can really level with" was a typical remark.

The following "syndromes" are not meant to ridicule. My goal has been to put in readable form the ways many clergy attempt to deal with low self-esteem and fear of human relationships. While the titles of each syndrome are my own, the content came from seminarians.

One of the most gratifying aspects of the work at Interpreters' House has been the privilege of seeing people gain self-esteem and engage in deeper relationships. They do become able to hear affirmation around them, and they do begin to change their style of ministry from functional to relational. Many a participant ceases being a functionaire to a small constabulary and begins to minister to the entire community. Participants' continuing relationship to Interpreters' House via letters, the Annual Convocation, and second-level seminars encourages us in this work and attests to the fact that what took place here was of lasting value.

PART I
Syndromes

Roadrunner

A common malaise of the clergy is the roadrunner syndrome. An automobile commercial once used a delightful cartoon in which a roadrunner kept up a mad pace across the country, running back and forth to avoid a coyote. The coyote was bent on devouring the roadrunner, but he was always outsmarted by the speed and cleverness of the bird. To press a point, the two never had a relationship anywhere near Buber's I-Thou, and it was certainly just as well, at least for the roadrunner. The roadrunner let no grass grow under his feet.

A minister who keeps moving, who maintains a frantic pace of production-oriented work, accomplishes, at least temporarily, two things. First, he affirms himself through function. His low self-esteem is (again temporarily) elevated because he is able to see what he has accomplished. I must be worth something he thinks, look what I've done. Measurable performance records are meticulously kept in his mind. He is keenly aware of the size and growth of his church membership, its budget, and the number of people who attend each meeting. He knows, and lets you know, how many calls he makes a week.

A year is always measurable because he knows how he's doing and what's been accomplished.

One polished practitioner of this art centered his attention on pastoral calls—the more the better. He began each morning by calling a list of his parishioners. If someone answered, he immediately hung up. If no one answered, he assumed the person was not home and that one was entered on his list of rounds for the day. He then moved out—to call on those temporarily absent, leaving a note at each door, thus getting credit for the function.

Another clergyman took pride in the number of organizations to which he belonged, paying particular attention to achieve some office in each. Still another concentrated all his energies on the budget. This particular pastor came to Interpreters' House morose because for the first time in his career, the current level of giving had dropped below that of the previous year. "It's the first time in my entire ministry this has happened," he said.

The roadrunner is convinced that his work is for God. "I want to be a workman who has no need to be ashamed," asserted one tired clergyman. "I haven't had a vacation in twenty years" was his battle cry. In reality, his labor is for his ego, and the demands of that master can be extensive and never ending.

The second thing the roadrunner accomplishes is avoidance of any meaningful relationships. He must keep moving. He cannot relax long enough to establish relationships and hence is protected from being found out. Believing that fundamentally he is not worth much, he functions not only to prove worth but to keep from being discovered as unacceptable. Loneliness and exhaustion are the result.

A person never affirms himself or herself by doing. It is impossible to gather enough trophies, because the more one has, the more one demands. Neither does one affirm oneself, by oneself. Escape from the syndrome begins with a willingness to risk honestly relating with a few accepting people. Once the trust level of a seminar begins to rise, deeper relationships are formed, and rather than the participants' finding themselves rejected, they discover a genuine affirmation. A participant may find that those around him accept him in spite of his "crimes" or his successes. He is accepted for himself—warts and all.

When someone begins to believe this affirmation, his attitude about himself starts to change. (Unless, of course, there are deep-seated psychotic reasons for his feelings of inferiority.) He no longer has to prove himself, either to himself or to others. His function can now become not a proof of being but an outgrowth of being. When he moves from the seminar experience back into the parish setting, he is more attuned to relating to others and is better able both to be affirmed and to be an affirmer.

Prayer for the roadrunner: Oh Lord, teach me that no good thing can sprout in a dust storm.

Room Service

When affirmation comes through function and sense of worth is determined by being a good and faithful functioner, it becomes extremely difficult to cease any function or to resist the call to a new function. A clergyman who feels compelled to function whenever called upon and is unable to deny any requests for his services becomes a victim of the room-service syndrome, that is, he becomes a lackey for anybody's need. When the call button is pushed, he—like the good hired hand—goes.

Much of the marital frustration in the clergyman's home (that I've dealt with) can be traced to this syndrome and has been the predominant complaint voiced by clergymen's wives.

For example, the Reverend D. plans to spend Wednesday evening with his family. His wife prepares his favorite dish. His young son gets the glove and ball ready to play catch with his father, and his daughter anticipates showing him two A's in math. He has not had an evening at home for some time and the family looks forward to this occasion. In the middle of the meal the phone rings—it always does. His wife tells him that Mrs. J. wants to speak to him. He goes to the phone—he always goes to the phone.

Reverend D.: Hello, Mrs. J. Nice to hear from you. (A lie, he can't stand Mrs. J., who is historically a manipulator of preachers and who always manages to call at suppertime.)

Mrs. J.: I've just got to talk to you. (She sounds urgent, but then she always sounds urgent.)

Reverend D.: Yes?

Mrs. J.:	The Women of the Church meeting today was terrible. You've got to do something about it. Could I come by in a minute—for a short talk? (They both know this is more a declaration than a question.)
Reverend D.:	Well, I—
Mrs. J.:	It will only take a few minutes. (Neither believes this. The last time, "a few minutes" ended up a rambling one and a half hours.)
Reverend D.:	Well, I was eating. (This has never worked before. Why hope it will work now? He will not assume the responsibility of refusing to meet. He hopes she will but in his heart of hearts knows she won't.)
Mrs. J.:	Well, if you don't think *my* problem is important—
Reverend D.:	Oh, no! [Oh, please, no. Whatever you do, don't think ill of me.] Come on by. I'll be glad to talk. (Second lie.)

Mrs. J. comes. Reverend D. is angry because she comes. His children are disappointed because she comes. His wife mutters her disgust at Mrs. J.'s thoughtlessness at staying two hours this time. (The reason she can't direct her hostility at the proper object, her husband, is because he has convinced her that the pastor's lot is a difficult one and that good stewards of the Lord are always on call.) Later he blasts his wife's cooking (transference—he dare not get angry at Mrs. J.), and the evening that might have made a blissful page of family togetherness in *Ladies Home Journal* becomes the cover of *Crime Drama*. Mrs. J. soars while the family circle has been shot down. Poor minister! He works so hard! Room service work is so demanding.

Let's see how this scenario might have gone:

Wife answers phone.
Wife: It's for you—Mrs. J. Do you want to come? (Wow! Who taught her that line? She knows he doesn't always jump through everybody's hoop.)
Reverend D.: Tell her I'm eating dinner. I'll call her back at eleven o'clock in the morning. (Dinner at home might be as important as Mrs. J.'s requests? Very courageous. He assumes Mrs.

	J. just wants to blast again and that one time is as good as another where her blasting is concerned. His promise to his family is more important. Note also that he has given her a time to blast. His time!)
Wife:	She says it's important. It's about the Women of the Church meeting.
Reverend D.:	Tell her if eleven isn't okay, I could see her at two o'clock. (Pause) What did she say?
Wife:	She hung up.
Reverend D.:	Oh well, she'll be okay in the morning. (Said calmly and without guilt.)
Wife:	Probably. You want some more peas?

The minister must budget his time, and time allotted for the family is important. There are calls that might have come to him that evening for which he would have been most willing to leave home. For example, if he had been notified of a death or of some other genuine emergency, he should have gone, and the family, while disappointed, would probably have understood. It takes a strong ego to discern when to interrupt a commitment (e.g., to be at home) and when not to allow it to be interrupted. By denying Mrs. J., he does run the risk of having her transfer to another church. She may brand him callous and indifferent, but he doesn't have to be loved by everyone. He acted with what he believed to be integrity and he will live with it. He selected priorities. The minister caught in the room-service syndrome cannot do this. Fatigue and chaos reign supreme.

Prayer for the room-service syndrome: Oh Lord, help me to distinguish between buzzers and sirens.

Dirty Guys Blew Up My Roadway of Life

The pastor's function is sometimes thwarted when his plans for increased membership, a new Sunday-school building, or whatever don't come off. Someone is to blame. The rage of his deprived ego then centers on the culprits. For example, a board member's honest question about the wisdom of an action the pastor plans for the congrega-

tion may be interpreted as a ruthless checkmate to his potentially ego-fulfilling function. "We would have had that new $100,000 educational building by now if Elder Doorjammer had only kept quiet."

Because successful function is imperative to ego satisfaction and relating is difficult if not impossible, plans are made in the secret confines of this pastor's heart, revealed at the proper (or improper) moment to the officers in the hopes that his "leadership" will be followed. If it is not, ego devastation follows, and in the attempt to survive what he considers a loss of face, blame is placed outside himself.

A pastor caught in this syndrome makes several erroneous assumptions. First, he sees himself as having superior goals and value systems (more Christian?) than his officers do—certainly more than the average church member. He believes that the good pastor convinces people what the will of the Lord is for his pet project. There can be no genuine "let us reason together" because his ego is on the line. For him, it's a win-or-lose game. For him, too, every idea is intimately connected to his ego.

When a minister believes basically in his own self-worth and is constantly able to receive honest affirmation in relationship, he is able to work with his congregation, and together they plan the work of the church.

Opponents and supporters need not be branded. Now they can be heard. Ego does not ride with every meeting; therefore, other leaders in the congregation can be developed without being a threat to self.

Prayer for the dirty-guys-blew-up-my-roadway-of-life syndrome: Lord Jesus, why won't I accept your omnipotence and my limitations?

Clean Blackboard

If measurable success is imperative and there appear to be no measurable successes, the clergyman may fall victim to the clean-blackboard syndrome. Its cry is something like this: "If only I could get a new slate of officers, I think things would begin to move." Or, "This church will never do anything, I can't wait to leave. If I had another church I'd show them what I could do."

Ministerial discontent is, I'm convinced, rampant. Every day somebody calls me wanting to move and hoping I might know of some ecclesiastical nirvana where he could start with a clean slate. Many are victim of the alcoholic's attitude though they are not actually alcoholics: If only the environment could be changed everything would be fine. A new church in a new town, a different denomination, another bishop, a more understanding district superintendent. While I do not deny that sometimes a change is in order, I am convinced that much groaning about situation is self-induced.

One seminarian, typical of others, was able to see that a valid but radically new form of ministry could take place in his small Southern town. When he discovered that most of his measures of self-worth and his concept of success were inauthentic, he could engage in fresh relationships. He became, in short, a minister to the region and not merely to a local confederate constabulary. The ministerial pecking order (How many members did you say you had?) was no longer a threat.

Prayer for the clean-blackboard syndrome: God, I confess that those folks aren't the problem.

I Must Be A Prophet, Else Why Are They Stoning Me?

Mark Twain once told a story of a man who was seized by a mob, tarred and feathered, and run out of town on a rail. When asked what he thought about this, he replied, "If it hadn't been for the honor of the durned thing, I'd just as soon have walked."

The clergyman caught in the prophet

syndrome would not agree. If there are no other measurable forms of success, his frustration may lead him to attempt to authenticate himself through persecution. A professor at a major seminary once told me that any preacher worth his salt will be hated by most of the town and the majority of his congregation. The word must have got around to other centers for theological training, because I hear this from a number of the clergy. The reasoning is this: Jesus suffered, prophets suffered, Paul suffered, Stephen suffered, et cetera. Hence, the greater the suffering, the greater the Christianity. Certainly anyone who sees beyond his region knows that authentic persecution of courageous folk takes place daily. Anyone who stands for truth that runs counter to well-entrenched cultural mores runs the risk of losing his head. This kind of suffering is not part of a prophet syndrome; it is real. The syndrome occurs when hostility is unconsciously, though deliberately, structured. It happens when suffering is seen as an authentication of one's own self-worth: to suffer is Christian; I suffer; I am Christian.

The clue to this syndrome came when I noticed in counseling with a number of men who had been under fire that actions they told me they had taken seemed to me obviously stupid. The furor that resulted from these actions seemed to please them. When I asked them about this, they protested vigorously the suggestion that they had perhaps been guilty of a wrong move or careless words. One participant noted for courageous preaching asked that I read one of his sermons. Even as I read the sermon (though I agreed with the issue he was challenging), its abrupt language and implicit sarcasm made me angry. He handed me the second sermon with a smile and said, "This one really infuriated them." It was clear that their response had pleased him.

Another minister came to me under the guise of seeking help, weary from his church's hostility. But it soon became apparent that he had come to tell me of his courage and to seek confirmation of his worth as a prophet. I asked him when the trouble with his flock began and he replied, "When I finally got up courage to tell Elder Grunch what I thought of that stained glass window his father had given to the church thirty years before." The day before this confrontation, the church's annual report had come out, showing a loss of membership.

By living under attack, he was able to see himself as a prophet (and a person) of worth.

After pointing out to one young theologian the prophet syndrome he had been using for eight years in the pastorate, his only reply was, "Just tell me this, do you think Jesus was well liked?" Every evasion can be covered by a so-called theological truth.

Prayer for the prophet syndrome: When I must face lions, oh God, let me at least hope their teeth aren't sharp.

Beef Jerky

A clergyman, under the guise of patience and humility, may allow himself to become the recipient of all forms of hostility without raising a cry of protest or a word in his own defense. The "stoned prophet" structures hostility, the beef-jerky victim is just that, a constant victim of any hostility that happens to be in his neighborhood. "Chew on me" is this syndrome's theme.

Here am I without one plea,
Come wipe your muddy boots on me.

All hostility must be called. That is, the recipient of the hostility must acknowledge to the dealer of hostility that hostility is transpiring between them. The recipient may choose to be patient and retain his anger, he may get angry in return, or he may respond in a number of other ways. However, no conversation can take place if hostility is ignored or totally absorbed by the recipient.

One seminarian told of an elder who would seek him out every Tuesday and "give him hell" for something in the Sunday service. The pastor would always sit patiently and listen, although usually he was furious. One week when the anticipated complainer arrived, the pastor said he could take it no longer and he told the man in very certain terms what he thought about these Tuesday tantrums. One-way communication ended and the possibility of relationship had begun.

If a pastor does not like himself very much, he will find the anger of others directed to him subconsciously affirming. It confirms what he really thought of himself—"I'm really not much." Or he may, as we have noted, believe that the good pastor accepts hostility without complaint.

Prayer for the beef-jerky syndrome: Oh Lord, help me to attract a few more healthy folks.

Court Jester

While I was doing some work with a large national sales company, I noticed one of their brochures of morale boosters for greater sales was headed with the caption "When In Doubt—Smile." It went on to say that of all facial expressions possible with the human face (over thirty-one—an incredibly high number it seemed to me), the smile was the most universally acceptable and the one likely to please the most folks. "Smiles hide frowns," and "humor is the best medicine," they counseled. I thought of all those times in my civic club when I was intimidated into singing "Smile and the World Smiles with You." This "medicine" seemed horribly out of place as I looked at it just after the second Kennedy was slain.

In working with several of these jolly-salesman types, I soon learned that behind the masked smile and generally jovial demeanor were many moods—fear, depression, anxiety, uncertainty—the whole gamut of human emotions. But, all they were willing to show was the pleasant persona. Even the Willy Lomans *looked* like Zorba the Greek.

Clergymen caught in the court-jester syndrome follow this pattern. They are always

pleasant. They smile a lot, often know a number of one-liner jokes, and are always able to meet any personal encounter with pleasantries and humor. In fact, the court-jester clergyman will never get angry.

Humor is frequently used as a defense against any kind of interpersonal relationship. It creates a buffer zone to keep from being discovered. Humor, together with social pleasantries, much smiling, and joviality mask real feelings. Those who have perfected this technique will smile when insulted and often laugh when being verbally attacked by another person. Laughter is used to deny the reality of any confrontation.

In one seminar (typical of others), a well-trained court jester infuriated the group by reacting to their hostility with a bland smile and his mimeographed line "No matter what you say, I'll love you."

Our seminars often provided the first place in the court jester's adult life where he was able to show anger and experience acceptance by the group. Other emotions soon followed, and the beginning of genuine relations ensued. He was able to discover that he could be himself—all moods included—and still be upheld by the group.

Prayer for the court jester: Jesus of Cana weddings and Nazareth graves, teach me when to laugh and when to cry.

Ha, Ha, Ha — Jab, Jab

This syndrome makes for an aggressively hostile court jester. Humor is used to hide, but it is also used to disguise aggression. It is a subtle form of attack. An example might be something like this: "Great suit you have, Charlie." (Smiles and laughter.) "If I hadn't given so much money to World Missions I'd be able to afford one like it." (More smiles and laughter.) One defense in kind against this money-oriented attack is to say, "Friend, you'd be surprised how your standard of living rises when you quit tithing."

Aggression in the ha-ha-ha–jab-jab syndrome is usually used to protect oneself from being found out. It is in the tradition of the West Point Manual, which states that the best form of defense is the attack. But it's also more. Often, people angry at themselves will lash out at others in a subtle form of transference. The cheapest way to exalt oneself is to debase another, goes the old adage. To do this openly would not be nice, so humor, as it were, excuses the attack.

In seminars where this occurs I usually ask the jabber to tell the victim what he really thinks in plain English. Why does he make you so mad? The hope is that we can then begin to deal with genuine feelings and that some more honest form of communication will result.

Prayer for the ha-ha-ha–jab-jab syndrome:

Lord Jesus, take away the smiles from my hostility and the sternness from my joy.

Cool Hand Luke

"Never lose your cool," a corporation president told a group of executives just before introducing me to them. My job was to get the participants to engage in honest dialogue with each other in order to build a smoother working relationship in the company. If they had followed his advice, our two days together would have been a failure. Fortunately, most of them saw his counsel in this situation as unreal and were able to be more honest with each other. In short, they didn't always play it cool.

The Cool-Hand-Luke syndrome is still popular with many members of the clergy. The victim of this syndrome has a facial expression as neutral as a death mask. There is no show of anger or laughter or sadness, nothing that would reveal genuine feelings. It is an almost blank expression. It is impossible to tell by facial expression what a Cool Hand Luke really feels since he always plays it cool. This protects the self from relationships that might hurt.

In a relationship in which someone knows how I truly feel, I become vulnerable. So, the mono-mask hides all.

Prayer for Cool-Hand-Luke syndrome: Oh God, help me to risk showing some of my warts.

He Walks with Me and He Talks with Me

While most clergymen I see are friendly with many people, they have few, if any, deep personal friends with whom they can share their real fears, desires, frustrations, joys, et cetera. Loneliness, as I have previously noted, is a common ministerial complaint. Low self-esteem and the fear of interpersonal involvement accentuates the problem.

Often, the clergyman will attempt to compensate by a vigorous devotional life of prayer and meditation. While I am in no sense making light of the devotional life, it can be and is sometimes used as an escape from relationship with persons.

One seminarian who was unable to communicate with anyone in the group defended himself by saying, "It really doesn't matter how you get along with people. It's how you get along with God that counts." After the session he came to me with a hymnbook and pointed to the following words:

> What a friend we have in Jesus,
> All our sins and griefs to bear!
> What a privilege to carry
> Everything to God in prayer!
> O what peace we often forfeit,
> O what needless pain we bear,
> All because we do not carry
> Everything to God in prayer!

"That's my theology," he said. "People often disappoint me. God never does."

Prayer for He-walks-with-me syndrome: Almighty God, hear my short prayers and discount my lengthy ramblings as escapism.

Street Urchin

Ministers are, for the most part, underpaid. The suburban pastor often finds himself in the lowest income bracket in his church. He often lives in a house he could not afford to rent, much less buy. He lives in a society not only affluent but a society that judges worth via pocketbook. But he does not make much money. How, then, can he resolve the conflict?

The street-urchin syndrome attempts to resolve the conflict by exalting low income. I made a list of responses from several men to salary questions in one week. Each of these ministers was married and had at least two children, and each had a total income, including benefits, under $7,000 per year.

"I could make a lot more money in any other job." This is sometimes true but more often naïve. Most do not know the job market. Others confessed that all they knew were Bible, books, and sermons, and, in fact, felt they could do nothing else but preach.

"Have you ever heard of a preacher getting rich?" Actually, yes, I have! But, the question is not one of poverty versus riches but of poverty versus sufficiency. It is comforting to many, though, to see financial struggle as synonymous with genuine Christianity.

"That's all they'll pay." Upon further questioning I discovered that none of those using this excuse had ever spoken seriously

to their officers concerning their expenses and needs. They had convinced themselves that the good pastor does not mention money except during an occasional sermon exhorting the members to give more money to the church.

"Actually, I don't get much money, but they do a lot for me." The whine for ministerial discount accompanies this. The praise of the church member who occasionally buys the minister a suit or gives him a good deal on a car is a part of it. Yet this all contributes to a dependency that is emasculating to many clergymen. However, to beg or to expect special favors from parishioners is usually a part of the street-urchin syndrome.

When a person's self-esteem rises and his sense of self-worth is enhanced, he can talk frankly to church officers about finances. When he is able to risk a genuine relationship with them and says what he really feels, he and the officers often understand one another as never before.

Prayer for the street-urchin syndrome: Lord Jesus, assist me to judge where I am and what I need without the help of modern advertising.

With-It-ness

A common way, particularly for a young member of the clergy, to establish a sense of self-worth is to be "with it." If one has the with-it-ness syndrome, one reads all the latest theological, psychological books, as well as the latest novels, whether one wants to or not. The with-it pastor experiments extensively with new forms of worship, often alienating much of the congregation; he attends the most popularized seminars, whether they are helpful or not; he uses the most fashionable language of the youth culture, even when the language does not express who he is; he wears the clothes that have just been introduced—in short, he is avant-garde through and through. The new is always replaced with the newer.

This creates pressure! Suppose this pastor meets someone who has read a self-understanding book that he hasn't read? What happens when he can't get free to go to that latest California touch session? How terrible when the church board rejects guitars two Sundays for equal time on the organ. How old-fashioned for them to be capsized by a dialogue sermon.

I am not lampooning new techniques or even the latest books. However, to always be obsessed with the latest thing is unhealthy, because one can never be quite that with it without undue pressure or abdication of congregational responsibility. Faith becomes fad. If a person is genuinely with it, he can reject the inauthentic. He can easily distinguish between the wheat and chaff.

Prayer for the with-it-ness syndrome: Carpenter Lord from Nazareth, cool my silly outlets for running scared.

Hark, I Perceive that Thou Art a Dirty Dog

We all have computer cards in our brain that have been programmed to evaluate people. These cards were punched out of prior experiences with all kinds of folks. For example, when you meet someone from the South who is short, slightly bald, wearing horn-rimmed glasses, and whose vocabulary has the flavor of a four-term Carolina senator, the computer cards might label this person according to information and prejudices stored earlier.

Since the evaluation is based on experiences with other people and not the person in question it is bound to be faulty. The psychological term for this phenomenon is transference. We tend to transfer experiences with one type of person to another, apparently similar type, even before a genuine meeting has occurred. If the transference is positive, it at least opens the way for an interpersonal relationship. However, if the transference is negative (unless the transference is recognized as such), no relationship is possible. If I perceive that thou art a dirty dog (negative transference), I am not likely to feel that a conversation, much less a genuine sharing with you, would be beneficial.

Clergymen, whatever their theological stance—from conservative to liberal or, as Carlyle Marney says, "from those with their windows stuck shut to those with their windows stuck open"—tend to have very rigid notions about what constitutes the religious person or the person of worth. The stereotypes are even stronger when black and white clergy meet. One of our tasks has been to insist that seminar participants "hear" each other through the negative transference. It has been exciting to see those whose negative transference inclined them to shun each other pursue the conversation to the point at which they could not only "hear" but learn and respect the other. Letters written a year or two after the time of a seminar tell us that this kind of experience carries over into the local pastorate. They begin to minister to more kinds of people.

Prayer for the dirty-dog syndrome: Lord of prostitutes and thieves, help me to hear and see beyond the obvious.

Plaster of Paris

Every church knows the kind of person a minister should be, and the expectations of every church are different. I recently received a letter from a congregation asking me to suggest the names of several men for their pulpit committee to consider. "We are looking for a man," the letter said, "who is young, a graduate of a Northern seminary, and slightly right of center." Another church asked me to suggest the name of a "liberal young man" and then proceeded with two pages of their description of this "liberal young man" spelled out in detail. Both congregations confessed they had had a number of problems with the last pastor because he was not what they had expected.

Every clergyman also has a model of what a clergyman should be. That model is an outgrowth of a minister known and admired or read about, or it may be the result of constructing a model from bits and pieces picked up in seminary. I've never met a clergy member who could not name an ideal model. Nor do I know of any seminary too timid to describe the ideal minister it hoped to see as the end product of its particular brand of theological education.

The result of an attempt to be a model is becoming impersonal. In trying to "be like him," the clergyman always neglects who he really is. For example, preaching that attempts to emulate an ideal always ends up as a distorted rendition of the original, and a textbook pastoral call never really leaves the library. The model hides the person from himself and his unique talents as an individual.

Conflict occurs when the clergyman finds that he is failing miserably in his attempt to be his model and feels guilty because he cannot attain his ideal. Conflict also arises when the clergyman's model is not the model the congregation wants or expects. To escape this kind of conflict, the minister often takes for himself a new model that is either less guilt-producing, more pleasing to the congregational idea, or both. He reshapes himself or allows himself to be reshaped like plaster of Paris whenever he moves into a new situation. He hums too often and to too many people, "Mold me and make me . . ."

Inevitably, more guilt and frustration result. He may feel that he has sold out to congregational expectation and that he must ever be on guard lest they find him out. When he sang "mold me and make me," the congregation did and he's embarrassed. He may feel that even the new model he voluntarily took for himself is impossible to achieve. In either case, there is often a longing to be himself but the inability to know who that might be. He has lived so long with his inner expectations or the outer expectations of his parish that self-discovery seems impossible.

Many seminar participants come with their announced agenda to discover themselves. I was surprised to hear so many confess, "I really don't know who I am." Often the appendage to this remark was, "I know who I *want* to be." They were clearly looking for a new model. I found that with many, their pattern of meeting group expectations was so ingrained that they merely substituted for congregational expectations, group ones. For example, several people in the group confessed to marital problems, but those with the plaster-of-Paris syndrome tended to confess their marital difficulties—real or imagined—in the hope that such confessions would make them acceptable to the others. They had perceived that persons could gain admittance to the group by certain kinds of confessions.

Freedom from the syndrome begins when group members become assured that there are no group expectations. The plaster-of-Paris victims who say and do things clearly for group approval are called, that is, the group itself says what it perceives is taking place. Freedom for the victim comes when he discovers that the unique life forces that made him who he really is can be acceptable both to himself and others. Indeed he learns that his style of ministry can be both unique and valuable because he begins to relate to people more and to function in less stereotyped patterns.

Prayer for the plaster-of-Paris syndrome: Lord Jesus, you know how good I am at running a mimeograph machine. Help me now to do my own typing.

Damascus Turnpike

Most denominations ask the candidate for the ministry if he or she has been called to preach. Sometimes a penetrating embellishment of the question is asked: "Do you feel as the Apostle Paul did, 'Woe is me if I preach not the Gospel'?" The appropriate and, in-

deed, only acceptable answer is yes. This reply is supposed to be followed by a detailed explanation. Not many "no's" make it through the meeting.

The purpose of these questions is to emphasize the importance of God's choice in the selection process. Only the Almighty can legitimately dub an individual fit to preach. Therefore, most candidates say they were called and know, within some limits, how and why they were called.

Most clergymen know exactly how God called them into the ministry, and more importantly they find their vocational authenticity in this divine call. After several sessions in which a middle-aged clergyman told me of the problem in his church, he added, "No matter what happens to me, I know God called me to preach." "In fact," he added, "my call is the only thing I am sure of." The Damascus-turnpike syndrome has two symptoms. First, the divine call to preach is the central and controlling theological experience in the person's life. It authenticates his vocation. Second, there is a refusal to even look again at the call for fear that it did not take place in the exact manner the person believes it did. An even greater fear is that it may not have happened at all. The call, then, is the foundation rock on which the Damascus-turnpike victim stands.

The clergyman's call frequently did not happen as he remembers it. For example, a boy of sixteen feeling guilty about what he thinks was a sexual "crime" (but which in reality was a normal occurrence for a teenager) gets the call to preach. Psychotherapy reveals that his real motive was to atone for his misconduct by becoming a minister. As an adult minister in the parish for some fourteen years, he has found that there is not much correlation between what he learned in seminary and the actual situation in the church. His seminary theology begins to crumble. "Maybe I was not ever called to preach," he thinks.

Freedom from the syndrome is achieved when the clergyman discovers that the manner of his call really does not matter. God uses whatever handle he can to get hold of a person. He learns that he can be the good servant even if he has not been originally motivated by lightning or by the still small voice.

Prayer for the Damascus-turnpike syndrome: God of Abraham, Isaac, Jacob, and Luther, motivate me to be a servant in spite of the absence of lightning.

Joan of Arc

A group of college and university chaplains inadvertantly gave me my first clue to this syndrome. I had been asked to lecture and do some psychological work for a foundation's annual meeting of its fellows, most of whom were university chaplains. In informal conversations with these folks, I often asked a few innocent questions to inquire about their work and to get conversation going—questions like "How's it going at _____ University?" and "Does anyone come to chapel anymore?" My conversation starters seemed to elicit from them almost a lament—from so many that their answers became more significant than I had anticipated: "The president, you know, is an ass. Really is! Lives in the nineteenth century. Doesn't give a damn about the students. [College chaplains cuss a lot.] All he cares about is raising money. The faculty is caught up in tenure and crap like that, though we have started a number of good discussion groups with them, trying to tie in with the students."

"We have started?" I inquired.

"Well, yeah, actually I tried to get the ball

rolling there by bringing them together. The first discussion was at my house."

"Great!" I reply, trying to sound casual.

"Well, they needed something. Just thought I'd start somewhere, you know. And the town—you probably know the town [I don't, but when people say "you probably" anything, I don't want to ruin it by confessing ignorance]. Backward as hell! I was asked to preach at First Church and, boy, were they shocked."

This may be enough to give you the theme: The president is unreal, the faculty is by and large a self-centered, calloused bunch, the dean's not much, the community is backward, the students have no support, et cetera. Implied is, Thank God I'm there to lead the troops to truth. God was sure lucky I could get free to accept this chaplaincy, and none too soon either. With me there, there's at least a beginning of truth and freedom and all good things—if only they wouldn't hinder me at every turn.

Since that college chaplains' seminar I've spotted the syndrome in clergy in other surroundings as well.

A clergyman in a one-industry town said, "This town is sick. It's been sick for one hundred years. But since I've come I've been able to—"

A cleric in a large suburban church said, "Why don't they listen? I preach the gospel and it just goes over their heads. They couldn't understand Jesus if he were to drop in some Sunday. I'm going to—"

A hospital chaplain said, "All these doctors care about is making money. I'm the only one who will really listen to a patient."

The Joan-of-Arc syndrome is not evidence of a strong ego head and shoulders above the crowd, standing for truth in an alien land. It reveals a weak ego, crushed and bleeding, trying to establish a sense of self-worth by allowing the self to develop a Walter Mitty fantasy. But the egotist never really believes his own propaganda for very long. He is afraid someone may discover the truth about him ("I'm not much"). He is pretty much a loner, although he always attempts to give the appearance of being a cut above these with whom he should be working—aloft and lonely. His inability to relate on a par with others forces him to relate only when he is top dog. He can talk to the college president only when he tells himself that he is superior in ethic and insight. He can preach only when he can show himself to be courageous and Christian, while the listeners are to be told what is truth.

Clergymen always for the underdog in the

community are often attempting to relate to those around them whom they believe to be inferior. For example, many white clergy who spend most of their time caring for the blacks may in reality be acting out a plantation orientation that allows them to look down on blacks while at the same time protecting their white egos. College chaplains who care only about the students may actually be relating to the only folks available who have fewer academic degrees than they do.

Prayer for the Joan-of-Arc syndrome: God teach me that I'm not as bad as I think I am—so I don't have to seem better than I am.

Et Tu, Brute

Trying to relate to anyone while expecting to have to dodge a fatal stab sometime during the relationship is defensive living that guarantees loneliness and anxiety. It's also a little crazy.

In one year I saw twenty-seven card-

carrying and reasonably successful clergymen toting defensive shields everywhere they went and wearing psychological-flak-proof vests. They were conducting their ministry expecting daily to receive some grievous wound to their career, reputation, and dreams by persons yet unknown. To these men, even the trustworthy were not to be trusted. They operated with the psychic stance of an alert karate expert on a jungle patrol who anticipates a knife from some dark quarter. They preached, visited, went to meetings, on guard.

Each of them had evidence to back up their attitude. I kept a list of one group's experiences.

Six years in the ministry: "I've got to watch my bishop. He's still out to get me for that sermon I preached last April."

Twelve years in the ministry: "All church officers I've ever had in my three pastorates hated preachers and tried to run them off."

Eighteen years in the ministry: "I moved North because all Southern towns are filled with hate. I've not found the North much better."

Twenty-two years in the ministry: "I keep my eye on all choirs I've had. There's something antagonistic about choirs. They'll get you if they can."

Twenty-three years in the ministry: "Why is it the women of the church are like they are? I don't trust them."

Twenty-five years in the ministry: "I told a district superintendent my problems once—I'll never do it again. None of them care about anything but their careers."

Each of the twenty-seven members of this group told stories of ex–good friends they had trusted who had severely disappointed them in some way. None of them had any close personal friends, and each of the contacts they now had with their congregations and community were shallow and merely functional. While none could have been said to be clinically paranoid, sometimes the distinction between paranoia and a low-threshold flinch response is small.

If one is rejected enough, one develops the tendency in any interpersonal exchange of anticipating rejection. The trick, or so some think, is to sniff out danger, anticipate alienation, and be the first to pull the knife. In other words, do it to them before they can do it to you. These people are like a cowboy who goes into a bar, draws, and guns down everybody only to discover that only the bartender had a gun and it wasn't even loaded.

In group sessions with clergy with the *Et tu, Brute* syndrome, it became evident that no matter how warmly disposed to me they felt, I knew they were looking for a flaw in my stance so they could say, "See, I told you so. I trusted you and look what you did." They knew at some time their leader would smash them. They were looking for rejection, and anyone who looks hard enough will find it.

One participant set up a request to see me at a time he knew was unreasonable, and when I refused his schedule for mine he told the group that I had really let him down. He added, "I'm not surprised."

Another kept sharing more and more of his "crimes" with the group—saving his big homosexual confession until the end of the first week. When no one was particularly shocked by this, he turned up the volume of his obnoxious behavior—bred of his disappointment at being accepted—that guaranteed many would find him a nuisance and a bore. He finally won. They told him to go to hell. He was relieved, though he had difficulty in settling on the chief Brutus. Finally, I was selected. "Even you," he sighed.

It is hard to stop living as a victim if you really are good at it. It's often easier being outside the city gates ringing the bell than inside eating a good meal in anticipation of someone poisoning your food.

Prayer for the Et tu, Brute *syndrome:* Oh Lord, I think I need glasses. They all look like Assyrians.

PART II

Confessions of an Ex-Holy Man

The worst five years of my life were spent in the pastoral ministry. From June 1956 until January 1962 I was minister to a small group of people, native Ozark folk, migrating Yankees, and others. I didn't like the marrying or burying or calling or counseling or preaching. But most of all I did not like myself.

Right out of seminary, with a fresh coat of theological naïveté, I pounced into the small village in Arkansas intent on preaching the gospel, that is, as it turned out, on making the people fit my new theology or else. My game plan was simple: I had been taught the truth and, by God (first said religiously; later, antagonistically), they would hear it, follow it, obey it! I had the key. So what if their locked gates to the eternal veracities were rusty? My good preaching and productive operation would oil them.

My training had been scholastically sound and functionally oriented. Study diligently every morning from 8:30 to 12:00, being certain to include sermon preparation, which in turn must include studies in Greek and Hebrew.

Good exegesis was expected, bad exegesis was inexcusable, and topical sermons were anathema. The afternoon was to be given to calling: those in need first (members only), prospective members second (always on the lookout for new recruits; only dead churches fail to grow), and if time permitted, social calls to members. I was equipped with sighs and "you feels" à la Carl Rogers of the fifties, Seward Hiltner handbooks, a knowledge of the Chester Beaty papyrus, and saddlebags stuffed with how-to-do-its. I knew the sixteenth-century heroes of my denomination and had waded through their intolerably dull writings for three years. I had studied Christian education in absentia from the real thing, knew the Hebrew alphabet, and believed in God. I was ready. Many years later I took a parachute jump and thought afterward of the similarity of the two experiences.

I was organized. My evenings were to be spent in meetings. The formula seemed to be: the more meetings, the more spiritually active. However, I dreaded the meetings, probably because I saw myself as a Holy Manipulator for good causes, that is, getting the elders and deacons to do what I knew had to be done. I soon came to see they had minds of their own, and I often left these encounters (they soon ceased to be just meetings) with a feeling of defeat and despair. I fantasized on what I could do if I just had another board. I understood stiff-necked people for the first time. But it took a while longer to discover my own narcissistic self-righteousness with which I was trying to cover my low self-esteem.

At first, all of my sermons were theologically correct—true to the text—with an ample dose of canned illustrations to make them palatable. I was a teller. I *knew*, they didn't; my job was to inform them. My first year's sermon theme could be summarized as "shape up, folks." I was not heavy on the "or else." I left that theme to the fundamentalists.

After a year, I ran out of anything scintillating to say. My pipeline to the heavens was getting clogged, that earlier rushing of a mighty wind spun down to a gentle breeze, and even that was not consistently on time on Sunday morning at eleven o'clock. I had preached all my seminary notes, everything I could remember from old copies of the *Christian Century*, and was down to faint remembrances of dorm discussions in which we played "Calvin Really Believed" and "Paul Taught" parlor games. I was dry. To make matters worse, the people were the same: the same troublemakers, and the saints (often those who agreed with me and supported my programs) were the same saints they had always been. We hadn't budged an inch. Still I droned on, preaching each Sunday about something. I tried diligently to cover the church calendar. "Give them well-balanced theological truth," one professor had told me. A series of sermons on the Holy Spirit, four on the Resurrection, eight dispersed through the year on sin, et cetera. It was very tiring keeping God and his word in a box on Sunday. But I had wound down from thirty minutes to twelve, while my prayers got longer.

My calling consisted of going to see the needy with the desire and chief goal of helping. Many years later, a friend in a seminar I was conducting told me the greatest sermon title he ever heard was "The Helping Hand Strikes Again." I knew what he meant. Some refused to be "helped," and I was left holding my anger (it was not nice to show anger openly) and my failure. I thought, I know what's good for them; why don't they do it? Even those rare instances when my visits seemed to be meaningful to them could be ruined if they did not later come to church. They had destroyed my ego game in which success meant church attendance. Who gets credit for helping? It's church attendance that counts. Got to get those numbers up.

Hospital calling was a particular torture. How could I compete with all those professional doers. One day in our small county hospital, I saw the Catholic priest take a picture of Jesus from the wall and go into a room. What *was* he doing I wondered. The door was ajar and I peeked in to see that the picture was a box containing the priest's extreme-unction kit. I envied him and I wanted one—something specific to do with dying. All I had done was stand around feeling awkward.

For a while, about seven months I think, I tried to pad my feeling of functional void by carrying religious tracts. I had narrowed them down to two, one was a short cheery paperback for the ill, designed as I remember to make the patient know his or her sickness did not have anything to do with an angry God holding a grudge against the person. It had a lot of vigorous psalms, a smattering of Pauline sufferings, and some eschatological hope passages. Handing it to the patient provided an adequate closing for a visit.

Another tract was called something like "Comfort for the Bereaved." I gave this one at funeral time to the survivors. It was a mass denial of the pain of death, and if taken seriously the grieving would have felt guilty for their grief. It implied that death was a nifty good idea God had, even if we mortals could not understand it. Get rid of your tears, it suggested; your dead loved one is having a ball. Most of all it helped me to feel I was again "doing" something.

I also had a small book on Christian family togetherness and worship. The cover had a picture of husband, wife, and two well-scrubbed children around a table with a flickering candle in the center. At this family worship center, patient father was reading the Bible, and the eager children showed the interest of kids watching Disneyland pass before their very eyes. Mother was pretty and domestic and devoted to God, her children, and her husband—in that order. I tried reading the Book, but it didn't work because my children just would not play their part. Finally I announced to my wife that I was willing to quit if she was. We were all relieved. Still, I handed the Book to others, heartily recommending it.

Even when I functioned successfully, my elation at having pulled it off never lasted. Sunday-school enrollment up by twenty-seven—I felt marvelous for five minutes.

"Sunday attendance is picking up," the old elder said to me.

"How much?" I asked.

"By about twelve a month," he said.

"Marvelous," I said. Now we've got to aim for twenty-four, I thought to myself. Every small trophy I got seemed to tarnish before nightfall, and I was off and running for a new one. Yesterday's quota had to be raised, and tomorrow's had to be higher than today's. We built a new educational building, and the night after the dedication I went into a blue funk that lasted two months.

After a year and a half, we started the second Sunday service, and I started sleeping late (avoidance, back to the womb), not calling on prospects, and stopping by the hospital only once a week. My weariness with functioning and my depression had married.

I can remember only a few instances of honest relation between me and a church officer during my entire time at that church. One was with Samuel, a "devout" deacon who used to crash my rare Mondays off with regularity to complain about me, my theology, my sermons, and my work in general. Each time with gnashed teeth I would patiently smile, toss phrases like "I take it you feel I've let you down," and try to keep my wish to kill and/or cry in check. One day I told him to shut up, and I was tired of his griping, and that I seriously hoped he would soon join another church. I later felt fresh and free. I had been honest. But that night I felt guilty.

In my ministry I lied a lot. I preached stuff I did not believe but wished to God I did. I smiled when I felt otherwise, tried to look adequate when I felt hopeless, and perfected a gift of gab that was cute, clever, and provided a smokescreen to hide in. I was lonely and acted as if I needed no one. I became a better artful dodger than the dodger himself.

The community respected me; the congregation tolerated me, many even liked me; and the denomination saw me as an up-and-coming young man destined to fill a decent-sized church if I would just hang in there, come to more meetings, and most of all keep the congregation growing.

I became an expert at producing and a rank neophite at relating.

It was a lot of years and therapy payments later when I saw that one of my principal creeds was "to know me—to really know me—is to reject me." So I kept moving to produce a few ego goodies and to keep from being found out. Those folks who wanted to get close were met by my keep-'em-off-base sarcasm or my self-sufficiency stares.

After four years, my schemes, dreams, ideas, and plans for the congregation were empty. My last year there I spent in trout fishing, hunting, and preaching on Sunday. I had decided to leave God's work. I turned on the vocation and accused it of being the enemy. Not one time in all that meandering down the White River did it occur to me that I was the problem. I concluded that I would do the only onward-and-upward-and-out thing I could think of. I would go to graduate school.

I would feed my ego in a new way with a new degree and another vocation. It worked for a while until I discovered that this plan had one gigantic flaw. I could leave, but I had to take me with me.

PART III
Rx — Maybe

Work Is Not Necessarily Moral — It's Just Doing

Relax and take down your scaffolding. If you don't build the Tower of Babel, someone else will.

When Ben Franklin's *Poor Richard's Almanac* invaded my part of the South, I thought it was good sound logic from a wise and prudent old man. The *Almanac*'s sayings commended hard work and staying productive with no nonsense and provided weather predictors to tell you when to do what. My hero dissolved when I ran into a volume of Franklin's letters written mostly from Paris when he was ambassador. I discovered that he raised hell, had quite a good time, dated, courted, and wooed the ladies with borderline abandon, and almost never lived by "A penny saved is a penny earned." I experienced the relief I had felt twenty years before when a neighborhood kid told me that he had it on good authority that Santa Claus really wasn't.

Later I heard the owner of a large textile plant tell my civic group the value of hard work and long days and make some comparisons between unions and Mephistopheles that made sense. It was such a good talk that I thought I should be doing something more productive than just listening. I ought to be getting with it. After his stirring speech, we talked informally and I found him to be a charming gentleman who wintered in Florida (forty-two-foot sailboat), went several times a year to the London theater, loved to hunt quail in South Carolina, and flew to the Bahamas (company plane) with the frequency of a 1920s rum runner. Oh, he believed in the value of hard work—for others—but he had not done any more than issue sound business decisions (valuable of course) to his board for thirty years. He was smart and he was clever, but he did not work very hard—and he didn't have to. Yet he thought and believed what he said about work and morality. He was sincere, and he was wrong.

Exhaustion may be the chief complaint of those ordained folks I see in group therapy. Tired, worn out from working so hard but never apologetic for treating themselves in such a shabby manner. Work to them is moral. "I've put in twelve to fourteen hours a day for the last two years," said one once bright-eyed young man of thirty.

"Any days off?" I asked.

"Very few," he said. "I haven't the time."

"Boy, that's dumb," I said. He was smitten. He had told me how moral he was (with a hint of his indispensability), and I had not only not appreciated his conscientious "worker in the vineyard" stance but had actually lampooned it. But then he was bragging and didn't know it.

Later, he shared with the group the fact that he didn't like himself. "I never have been much," he said. He attempted to produce work thinking it equivalent with morality. So much work equals so much morality, which in turn equals so much self-worth. When you are so tired you can't go on, you are at your most moral, or so he thought.

Everybody functions and everybody produces and most people work at something. Even the paraplegic who functions at a minimum still functions—still "does." One of the silliest outcomes of the insight craze is a person's saying, "I won't *do*. I'll just *be*." Try it and you'll never eat another apple.

It's not doing and producing that is in itself a trap. The trap is thinking that only doing contributes to worth as a human being. When excellent doing means I'm an excellent person and bad doing or not much doing at all means I'm not worth much, I've been had—by me.

We can use the circle below to indicate the relationship between a pastor and the tasks to be performed. If the arrows are going out from the *I*, a pastor, toward the functions, there is no problem with exhaustion or other common pastoral strains. *I* have control of what I do. *I* pick and choose my tasks. I function.

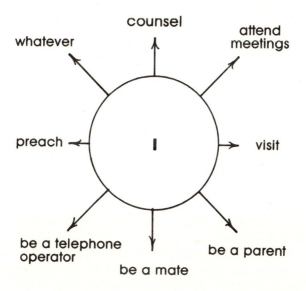

Exhaustion is the result when the arrows are reversed. When the *functions* give worth and validity to the I. Instead of *I do*, doing *does me*.

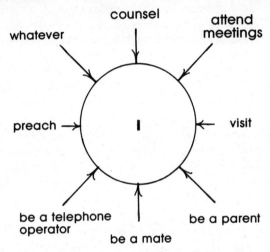

When the arrows are pointing inward, it means that every well-done function contributes to my sense of worth. It also means that any bad function is not just a failure but a defeating erosion of my ego. That's why after hearing ninety-nine times "It was a good sermon," it takes only one "You didn't have much to say today, preacher" to make many pastors have sleepless nights. The hungry ego demands function upon function because each one has the potential of feeding the ego and making ego feel worthwhile.

Work is only work—not in itself moral or immoral. Production is only production—not in itself moral or immoral.

After making the above statement to a group of clergy, one man protested, saying, "My work is moral because it's God's work. God's work is different."

"You mean," I asked, "that every week when you run the mimeograph machine, fix the coke box, and put out chalk for Sunday school that that's noble work?" I wouldn't let him answer and forged ahead, hitting him with information he had earlier shared with the group.

"Do you really think that's noble, or do you do it only because you haven't found anyone else to do it?"

"By God," he said (reverently), "I've run my last mimeograph machine!" (These instant conversions are rare.)

Much work people do is miserable Volga-boatman stuff, pulling the barge, hating every minute of it, motivated only by a paycheck. You may elect to do some grimy stuff just to keep your job secure, but don't label it moral just because the church pays you.

You may have ego needs that push you to visit *all* the sick every day (even those who obviously feel uncomfortable when you come in, giving signs such as pulling up the sheet, looking at the wall, and glaring at their watch), but just because you carry a cross (or a star) don't print "moral" on your T-shirt. Even you don't think it's so lofty an enterprise, do you?

To paraphrase Paul, even doing, doing, doing, won't do it. Your work may just be wheel-spinning that makes you feel better about yourself. Kicking up dust isn't necessarily moral (or immoral); it's just kicking up dust.

So quit working so hard and have some fun. No, you won't become an irresponsible slob or a beachcomber. You're bragging again; you haven't got it in you to go that route. You can trust yourself more than that. Take some days off and you'll dispel the myth that you're invaluable. The congregation will get along pretty well without you.

The world can run fine on your Monday absences. You might even try playing on Saturday, too. It may be somewhat disappointing to see that you're not the navel of the universe or your denomination or your town or your church. But it will be liberating nevertheless to no longer play God. It is very relaxing to be an average member of the species.

Pleasure Is Better than Pain?

Given a choice between warm soapy water for my feet and boiling oil, I'll choose the soapy water every time.

One day at the hospital, a pediatrician asked me if I wanted to make rounds with him. "There's a burn case you might find particularly interesting," he said.

"No thanks," I said. "That kind of grief I just don't need today."

When I related this to some clergy in a group I was leading, they all said they would have gone. "Why?" I asked. The answers varied. Some were curious. Another had never been with a doctor making rounds before and it sounded to him like a potentially interesting experience. But one reply I remember vividly, "I would have gone," one said, "because I grow with grief." "Growth through adversity," he continued.

"What do you mean?" I inquired.

"Well," he said, "it would have been a sad experience to be sure, but through facing that kind of ordeal I grow as a person."

"Hm," I mused to keep from saying, That's absurd!

Yet he probably spoke for many who imply, show me blood—mine or theirs—and I'm a better person for the experience. Our discussion continued and the others, gaining strength from the courageous stance of the "growth-through-grief" reverend, turned on me.

"You chickened out," one said.

"Yeah," quipped another, "you ran from life."

"You're right about the running." I said. "I eagerly avoid seeing pain and I'd do it again."

"But why?" they asked. By now they had become a chorus.

"Because it wasn't my grief," I explained. "And not only that, I had some fun planned for the rest of the morning—lunch with a friend and a swim in the pool and a good book. When I have the choice (*when* I have the choice), I choose pleasure every time."

The group chorus could not cover their disappointment. How sad that their leader should be such a hedonist. They seemed to view me as an Ivy League Bacchus, slurping wine, eating grapes, cavorting, totally immersed in pleasure, while the real world of sadness whirled about my selfish head. How dare I choose fun when I could have chosen tragedy and growth? Just imagine how I would have been strengthened by seeing a burned child in pain. Instead I wasted the day. I had a good time. (The grief-and-growth seekers would say Michael Servetus blew his chance when he escaped from the Inquisition the first time around. He could have been burned at the stake months earlier than he was.)

Where I grew up, the phrase "pleasure-seeker" was always equated with irresponsibility and selfishness and directly attached to irreverence. I wonder why.

I wonder why no one ever spoke to me about growth through pleasure? I am amazed that fun connoted "watch it," while pain was always noble, particularly if you liked what it ultimately did for your personal growth.

There is, of course, growth through adversity but only if it is *my* adversity and not some I manufactured or took a detour to find. Cross theology should be about those countless crosses (personal suffering experiences) that are in every human's path at various points in life. These are unavoidable. I had better confront them. Running does not help.

I once had a patient who said he thought he'd be all right if he could just go to Florida, walk the beaches, and have a ball.

"Sure you would," I said. "For a while!

Then you'd have to face the pain all over again. The running wouldn't cure anything." I cannot legitimately and healthily avoid any adversity in my path. I can, however, avoid those problems and sufferings that are not on my road. How foolish for me to look for wood and nails and Romans and search for an abandoned hill on which to construct extra crosses. How foolish to rush madly about going to cross parties, sipping gall, thinking the casual observation of pain is my growth.

Every year a number of people come to me with genuinely mind-boggling, though solvable, hurts and problems and confusions. Some of these folks convince themselves after one or two sessions that the things they were wrestling with really were not there at all. They seek to avoid the pain and expense by constructing a temporary illusion: things aren't so bad. Most of them return after six months because denial did not work.

Most people handle their grief experiences and suffering pretty well. We have all seen people who have been through it and we have marveled at the way they have survived with dignity and grace intact. I have often said, "I don't see how they did it," and I mean it. How indeed!

One of the ironies of our culture is that we are trained largely to produce and work and suffer to the glory of God or to the glory of the GNP-Wall-Street ethic, and no one told us how to have a good time. In fact, we were taught that a good time was only to be had after we took out the garbage and fed the dog and even then, "Don't play too long 'cause there's work to be done."

The friend who related the above remark to me said he once asked his mother, "What other work?" She said, "I'll think of something. You don't ever see me rest do you?" And he hadn't. Already the seed had been planted; play is frivolous. Doing unpleasant tasks builds character. My friend also said that he was forty-two before it hit him that he had not learned any good thing from emptying the garbage on time, but that he had learned a great deal from time spent bouncing a ball against the barn.

<u>Even pleasure in our country has to be productive.</u> Goofing off produces guilt, so we tend to avoid it by organizing productive pleasure.

A nine-year-old friend once asked me to go to the opening of his little-league baseball park. I was glad to go, and except for the speech given by the we'll-prevent-juvenile-delinquency leader it was fun. One line from the speech still rings, though. The speaker said, "If it weren't for organized sports such as little league, these boys would be wandering around throwing rocks and riding their bikes."

What's wrong with that? I thought. But there was no one to say that to.

There's a large lake twelve miles from my house, and one of the weekend folkways of my area, for those who can afford it, is hitching the boat to the car and going to a hidaway on the shore. The weekend pleasure-seekers ski or fish or work on the house or do something that's thought out and well planned beforehand.

I was asked to meet some friends at their cottage one Saturday, and I showed up with a six-pack and some magazines, found a shady spot on the deck, and proceeded to scan articles, snooze, and enjoy what could probably be called a low-key meditating. The other guests, who had arrived earlier, were engaged in serious water-skiing, serious fishing, serious sunbathing, and serious painting. My lounging was continually interrupted by little messengers dispatched by their parents to inquire if I didn't want to go water-skiing now. ("Daddy said to ask you.") Or didn't I want to go fishing or—?

My reply became monotonous. "No thanks, I'm just fine."

After two hours of weary kids trudging up

the steps from the water to ask again, the parents lost faith in the messengers and began to come themselves.

"Are you sure you're having a good time?" was the theme of their inquiry.

"Don't you want to do something?" was the embellishment.

They found it impossible to believe that my unorganized sitting could be enjoyable. When we all reassembled for dinner, two buddies asked me quite seriously if I was feeling ill. How ironic that doing nothing much can be so refreshing and the obligation to produce can be so wearying. I felt much better than they did.

Look at the ways we ruin sheer pleasure with the compulsion to make it productive.

Swimming:	"I really ought to learn a new stroke or practice my dive."
Reading:	"I enjoyed that book, but I ought to read more books to improve my mind."
Marvelous music:	"I'm so dumb I can't discern Bach E Fugue from the F. I ought to take a course."

Watching the clouds float by:	"I've got to learn to meditate better—maybe that guy from India—"
Reading the paper on Saturday morning:	"Ought to paint the garage!"
Super party:	"I don't think there was one prospective member (or client or customer) there. Just wasted my time."
Lying on the beach in the sun:	"Ought to call the office."
Great art museum:	"I really am stupid. Still can't discern all of Van Gogh from some of Cezanne."

When I was going through a particularly difficult time adjusting to the forties period, an architect friend of mine (my personal free therapist for the year) said to me, "You really have a hard time giving yourself permission to be happy, don't you?"

I hadn't thought I had, but he was right. My checklist had included everything but permission to enjoy myself: (1) face problems directly; (2) be responsible for my life and stop acting as if I'm responsible for the world's happiness and/or sadness; (3) confront what I want for the remaining time I have left to be a sensitive human; (4) strike some sort of balance between my chicken nature and my brave Viking in the prow of the ship of illusions. With this list, I had unconsciously (perhaps consciously) given pain priority over happiness. I discovered numerous ways in which on my brightest best days I could introduce gloom. I remembered an autumn day backpacking in the Smokies when the sun was reflecting the colors and the air was clear—how wonderful. At the peak of this experience I went through one of my pain checks: Have you really been a good father? Is what you're doing fair to your children? I felt relief when it started to rain and the clouds moved in. I had muddied my day. I hadn't given myself permission to be happy. <u>The pleasure was uncomfortable, so I carried a cloud in my pocket just in case.</u>

I also recalled the time I had splurged on lobster and a nice bottle of Brauneberg Riesling. Just as the feast was in full swing I had decided to ask myself if I should have been more frugal because my daughter in college could have used the money. I had ruined a good meal by checking my responsibility. Of course I was a responsible person, and I'd already made good decisions about tuition and expenses. I just wanted to ruin a good thing. Permission to be happy? Not often given and not for long.

It was an embarrassing but freeing experience to see those many times when I actually had the option of having a good time or a less than good experience and had dialed "less."

It was not easy to quit; my hallucinations were haunting. Calvin seemed to stare at me. Immanuel Kant made speeches to me about Duty. My mother frowned one of her deep sigh frowns. My children looked hungry and forelorn. All my imagination! I asked Calvin to leave and he smiled, so I told him it was okay to stay. I was ready to shoot Kant between the eyes, but he quickly admitted I knew more about Duty than he did. My mother quit sighing as soon as I quit flinching. My children didn't even know what I was talking about because they were having a very good time with their friends.

You actually can give yourself permission to enjoy life more than you do, and only you can do it. How egotistical of you to choose to be the second-best suffering servant.

The Narcissistic Cowboy versus the Holy Mob

Knowing who you are and discovering your own unique personal identity can be lost by the acceptance of one of the two myth systems in our culture.

One is the loner myth of American individualism, sometimes "rugged," sometimes withdrawn but always lonely. The true individual, so the tradition says, does his own thing no matter what anyone thinks. He feels best when in opposition to others, and he lives in constant fear that some movement, some subtle universality, will gobble him up and he'll be lost forever in the crowd.

Early on, this phenomenon is seen in the rebellious five- to six-year-old child who finds identity by kicking and screaming at parental authority and saying no obstinately only because his mother says yes. In its middle-age incarnation, the myth may produce the prosperous self-made man who believes he did it all—factory and Mercedes—on his own, forgetting that somewhere someone cared for his irresponsible posterior and held the bottle in his mouth. In its best religious form, the myth is represented by Micah or Amos and in its worst, by the lonely cynic, who sneers his way through ecclesiastical gatherings poking fun at the denomination.

The other extreme myth is the image of the corporation man—or, if you will, sometimes the good churchman, good presbyter, good conference worker, good company man, whose personality and individualism is smeared into that of a group. He is the one whose joining means he submits to the company or confessional value system and forgets anything personal. He sings the club song, wears the uniform, buys the rules, believes the creeds, rarely rocks the boat, and knows that dissent is not nice. Who he is, is defined by what the group believes. His questions are the group's questions, and its beliefs are his beliefs. He gets his identity by emulation, and he is a good member of the mob. Whether sacred or secular, a mob is a mob. A mob's members have submitted all individual identity to the crowd. When this happens, all personhood is dependent on the group, and the logo can be corporate seal or cross or star or badge. It's still a mob.

My neighbor here in the mountains demonstrates his tension between individualism and group identity well (though I doubt if he would admit it). At the entrance to his driveway he has two signs, one reading "United we stand, divided we fall" and a second, smaller one, hastily stenciled, says "Private Drive—Keep Out." And over his half-acre plot flies the American flag.

I grew up with the superior cowboy as hero. The lone cowboy on the lone prairie astride an extremely intelligent horse, his saddlebags carrying beef jerky and beans, his bedroll at hand to insulate against chills, a yellow poncho to ward off rain, Colt-45 on his hip, and a Model 94 Winchester in a saddle scabbard. He was self-sufficient, brave, unique, able to live off the land (they don't pay me much but I like church work), flexible to variations of terrain and climate (meeting with the district superintendent; Annual Conference time), needing only a now-and-then night on the town (haven't had a real vacation in years), a trip to the general store (book store), and an occasional visit to some good female listener (faithful wife rarely sees me). A loner!

The theological cowboy carries his ninety-five theses wherever he goes and sometimes nails them up for effect (brave individualism). No quorum will make him change his mind. If he is ordained, he may think of himself as a prophet, while his denomination sees him as a nuisance. He is lonely but often reports to his wife his latest misunderstood prophetic sycamore thrust into the heart of Jerusalem or Baal. At best he is narcissistic, and at worst he is a religious sociopath.

The corporation clergyman stands for group truth. He digests creeds and confessions and church order with gusto, believing its historical, voted-on food nourishes him. His stance is defined by a group value system. He is lost without the crowd.

Both these extremes guarantee loss of self and both are slavery. The loner is locked up in his personal cell with the key in his own pocket. The groupie gives his company or denomination the key and asks what time the meals are served. Both have appeal nevertheless.

Any relationship can be painful, and individualism at least protects you from vulnerability that is a part of any honest relationship. Most loners, I think, have earlier been hurt by people. Perhaps as a child, they reached out to hold someone's hand and that person was too busy to hold it. Or later, out of a hope that all people would be nice if they were nice to everybody, they ended up getting taken. Being done in by another person is not anyone's exclusive experience. We have all been had if we have related to people at all.

Not long ago I did a series of group sessions with people who are either divorced or separated on the way to divorce. There was no attempt to salvage any marriages because it was too late for that, and one of the ground rules for admission was to recognize that the marriage was over. I was amazed to learn that only one of those attending any of the groups had initiated the divorce. It had all, they thought, been done to them. They came wounded and angry. "I never will trust that way again" was their theme. By talking together they were robbed of their claim of exclusivity in being shafted. They talked of distrust but trusted enough to tell it. They learned that a certain amount of gullibility is necessary for any intimacy between people. They probably moved on with their lives, trusting, I hope, with a bit more discernment.

The clergy I see are often lonely because they have lost their innocence. They have put aside being wise as serpents and harmless as doves for being just lonely birds. They have forgotten or never learned that you can trust some people and some people you can't and favor instead the maxim that declares none are to be trusted. They are angry that they do not live in a well-run schoolhouse, with a kindly schoolmarm, and nice little boys and girls. They long for a cause-and-effect universe and a church that has only good folks.

I experienced a sense of relief when one of my teen-aged daughters told me she had learned that all boys were not to be trusted. It was a greater relief to see she did not quit dating but went on to exericse some discernment. <u>Some fins in the water belong to dolphins and some belong to sharks</u>. One can't always be sure, especially from a distance.

Joining the corporation of God, whatever the label, has its advantages. Most holy mobs I see reward their followers with a paternalism that is well structured, concisely organized, and poorly paid but that guarantees a certain amount of insulation from the real world.

The Son of man may have no place to lay his head, but the good corporation clergyman usually does if he follows the rules, and they are simple:

1. *Be good*. Drinking and smoking sometimes, depending on the denomination. Sexual prowess or perversity never. Being good is secondary to looking good. If it looks good, it is good.

2. *Work hard*. This means not only working hard but looking as if you're working

hard. Act busy. Looking frantic, if punctuated by deep sighs at meetings helps. Increased membership is always proof you are working hard. Spiritual growth might be, too, except it's too hard to measure.

Included here is being religiously ambitious, which is no different from being IBM ambitious except you say it's for the sake of God. All God's servants want to get ahead—or should. Don't look for a biblical precedent: this part is American Gross-National-Product ethic. If this bothers you, remember to be American is to be Christian.

3. *Be faithful.* Here the denomination defines what it means by being faithful. Churches vary, but this always includes the core of the rule book. Never fear—the church will tell you what the core is. Remember the faithful go to the meetings and vote yea. You are allowed to attack some denominational policy once a year provided it is done in the name of God, and more importantly for the good of the denomination. When in doubt about this, always look back to historical precedents, never ahead to social change. Everbody knows the value of hindsight.

Here's the formula:

> Being good + working hard + being faithful=People will like you (and

even if they don't, the denomination will). You will always have a job and a sense of belonging. You will be able to live your life in well-defined parameters.

This is paternalism at its best.

In either individualism or corporate sell-out, the person is missed, human fulfillment is avoided, uniqueness is lost, and loneliness is accentuated. Despair and frustration often go along for the ride. There are alternatives I think, to these extremes.

First: relation. Everyone needs three or four people to whom he or she can be honest and open and candid about everything. To have more than five is greedy.

These are people you have met along the way with whom you confess and celebrate, weep and laugh, and no matter what you say or do, they will not cast you out. You share with each other anything you wish without fear of being rejected.

These people are also your correctors, and you are theirs. They do not just hum the "Hallelujah Chorus" to everything you do or say, because there is no true affirmation without the occasional "You really were a jackass." When you say you acted stupidly, they probably will agree, but they won't send you to your room without supper. They are friends, and in spite of anger, agreement, or disagreement they remain friends. You do not always praise them, nor they you, but when it's damning time you don't have to hit the road and find another set of people to whom to relate.

There is a movement now afoot usually called support groups. It is one of the latest psychological-theological fads. I get the impression that a Wednesday meeting is called, which means it's relating time at the old corral.

"Time to relate, folks."
"Let's all be honest."
"My, my, that wasn't so bad, was it?"
"Yeah, I know how you feel."

It's an improvement over the idea that we have to feel one another's nose and break out of the circle to be mentally healthy, but not much of an improvement.

Most support groups with which I'm familiar are too canned. They reflect too much the old organization ethic that says, "We've got a problem: let's have a meeting." Also, I just never have liked to relate on demand or to be intimate on call.

The handful of potential friends I'm talking about may or may not ever meet as a group. They may not all ever live in your town and they may or may not have a party together, but they certainly will *never* call a relating meeting. One or two may be in your church, in spite of the advice most of us were given in seminary not to ever have special friends in our congregation and to treat everyone equally.

You find these people where you find them. It is naïve and limiting to hope for them all to happen to be in your vocation or in your neighborhood or in your age group. They are all around you. Just look. They are probably as frightened as you and as hungry as you for someone to be real with.

Second: the group. Anyone who works for any organization or pact must submit himself or herself to certain disciplines and procedures and purposes of that group.

Maybe you were tolerated that first day or two in kindergarten when you kicked and screamed at everything that went on, but eventually you learned to hold the crayon, find the bathroom, and follow the schedule. You did not lose your identity or feel that you had sold out, did you?

Ultimately, no club or clan will tolerate your daily desire to rewrite their manual; nor will they permit you to ride your horse through their parlor shooting out the lights

<u>and gunning down their authority figures, and they shouldn't.</u>

The ability to accommodate or get out is necessary. Most people spend much of their time doing things that are not fulfilling or fun but are required. So what? If you have to defend your personal integrity at every turn, the chances are you do not have much. You don't defend that which is not up for grabs.

If I'm going to join the pack, and everyone joins some pack, I've got to play by some of their rules, even those that are time-consuming and dull and those that I think have no merit.

Certainly there may be some requirements that one cannot and will not accept. But for most folks, they are fewer than they originally thought. On the critical issues, creeds, schedules, or conditions I can fight for change, risk my job, and maybe win. If I win, fine. If I lose, I can resign. Every job ought to be done with an updated signed letter of resignation in one's pocket. There may be some things one will not tolerate; nor does one have to. There may be others one will smilingly perform, knowing the task is silly but knowing also that to belong means to play some of the games.

The Relief of Being Average

Anything worth doing is worth doing average.

So many people absorb sometime early the idea that they were born with a deficit in character value. They think of themselves as below par—inferior. A young man told me that on the day he left the farm and a passel of brothers and sisters to go to college his father said, "Be somebody. Anybody can be nobody."

He said that the interpretation he put on the advice of his father was, "You're not much now, but work and study hard and someday you'll be a decent, qualified person instead of a nobody dirt farmer like me. You're nobody now, but education will fix it." It hadn't and he was depressed.

Most people have been told in some form or another that their present being was unacceptable, but if they worked on it, they would eventually be qualified to join humanity. Messages were constantly being sent, usually by osmosis, that they were inferior. No speeches were made, but the idea was in the air. Onward and upward was the theme song playing in the background.

It is ironic that well-intentioned parents often send daily messages to their children that imply the child is stupid, irresponsible, weird, rebellious, frivolous, lacks decision-making capabilities, cannot speak without mistakes, et cetera.

Child	Parent
"I want to go camping with John."	"Can't you see it's raining?" (Dumb idea, kid. You're so stupid you can't even discern rain from sunshine.)
"I've got a date with Bill to the prom—wow!"	"Oh no you haven't. Not unless he cuts his hair." (Don't you know how to pick friends?)
"I made a B in algebra."	"You're capable of making A's." (Nothing less than perfect is acceptable, and you're certainly not perfect.)
"See the frog I caught."	"Yok—ugh! Why don't you play with your dog?" (You can't even pick pets.)

"I want to be a carpenter when I grow up."

"Okay. But you're going to college first. Don't forget that, young man." (You've got to make more of yourself than that. You're too stupid to pick your own vocation anyhow; I'll do it for you. Even if Jesus was a carpenter, that was another time.)

It is not my intent to give a discourse on how to raise children. I've raised two and in many ways I'm still an amateur, and on bad days I have some trouble in facing myself for my inability to be a better (do I mean perfect?) father. Nor am I intending to attack parenting, though the effect may be the same thing. I am suggesting only that the message many of us received from loving parents was "You're not much now, but if you work real hard, someday you might. . . . !" The assignment was Be Superior (perfect?), and you can be if you just keep working at it.

But how? By climbing, achieving, progressing daily, getting ahead at least semiannually, improving, polishing, producing. Degrees, certificates, money, better job always on the way to an even better job, more security, better friends, greater sermons, bigger churches; the list was and is endless. Achieve nirvana was the command. We don't know where it is but its somewhere up there in the clouds—you'll find it. You must find it. You're inferior.

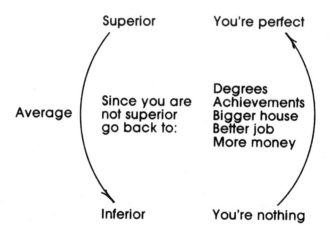

A top executive from an international company was depressed. He was tired all the time but couldn't sleep. He said that he didn't know what it was to not work hard. "I've never relaxed and had fun in my life."

He found himself crying a lot, and he had not cried in years. He saw himself as a failure, though by external measurements he was a success: money, position in the community, responsible job, charming and devoted wife, two well-adjusted kids, and one not so well oriented.

He told his story about clawing his way out of a Georgia farm, how he discarded bib overalls for custom-made suits, and how he had acquired prestigious degrees from Ivy League schools. He had made it. But to himself he hadn't.

"I keep making mistakes," he said. "I'm not there yet, and I'm tired." He had pulled it off, but he still felt inferior.

("Where is up?" asked the traveler. "Keep going, you'll find it," said the sage [who looked remarkably like my grandmother].)

There was a bishop who even in the hospital gown stood as if he were fully robed and mass was about to begin. He had thought being bishop would fix it. It hadn't.

Another had just been accepted as a full member of the conference—a desire he'd had for years. Limited education had kept him patiently waiting for years in the wings of his denomination. But through finesse, more education, a good record, and political skill he had been admitted to full participation. He felt lousy.

My own depression hit after eleven years of

school. A Ph.D. would do it, I believed. It hadn't. I was still inferior. Where do I go from here?

It took three months for me to make the appointment with the psychiatrist. I would pick up the phone and put it back in the cradle (one month). Then I would dial the first three digits and hang up (two weeks). About eleven times I dialed the number and quickly pushed the button down before the receptionist had time to answer (six more weeks). When I finally let it ring, I hoped there would be no answer.

I had decided I would tell him all my crimes in first session and so I did. For thirty minutes I poured out every crime, every hurt, every failure I could remember. He didn't flinch. Surely he had not heard much worse in all his practice. Surely he'll get up and depart or ask me to leave. Instead, he listened with a mixture of interest and boredom, or so I thought. When I paused for breath before listing more of my misdeeds he interrupted me, "I don't care about *that*," he said. "Get on with it." That was my first conscious recollection that I didn't have to be perfect. It was my first experience with "grace." The word was often used in seminary, but it's hard for us achievers to hear it.

As our sessions continued, he gently reminded me that while we were both in agreement about my failure to be superior we still faced another problem.

"Well," he said. "You tried to be perfectly superior and that didn't work, did it?"

"No," I said, eager to affirm what we both knew to be true.

"Now," he continued, "you're trying to pull off being *perfectly inferior*. Why don't you just make peace with being *average* like me."

Average, I thought. That's the most vulgar word either of us had used, and we had used a lot of vulgar words.

Anyhow he's not average. He's a psychiatrist. God, I envy him.

"Look," he said. "I tried being God for six years and I had to give up. You did, too. You just didn't make it. We both agree on that. Anyhow, being God is so demanding. This perfection stuff is a lot of hard work. Why don't you first settle for average?" (I flunked again.)

I loved superiority, but even when I felt superior it lasted only a short time and anyhow I never really believed it. One negative comment from any passerby could dethrone me.

I didn't like inferiority either, or I wouldn't have labored so long to work my way out of it.

Why then was I so insistent on viewing myself as inferior? Because inferior was at least consistent. I could go into a meeting and always have a prize. So what if it was the booby prize, and so what if it was self-awarded? It was better than nothing. I was bragging in reverse.

It never occurred to me to make peace with average. It was worse in my mind than inferiority.

Nobody wants to be average, I thought. I had bought the cultural brainwash that drones incessantly, You can do better than that.

Of course I can, but where does it stop? When can I get off this achievement wheel and get some rest?

One of the dirtiest words in our culture is "average," and it gets knocked out of us early. The Holy Word seems to be "superior." The cathedral is "improvement." The hymn is "anything worth doing is worth doing well." The motto is "second to none." The ultimate product is despair.

Eleven-year-old Charlie brings home all C's on his report card, and he's immediately sent to his room to get with it. Later, his parents make an appointment with me to see if the horror of their suspicions could be true.

Could it be possible that this urbane, well-educated couple has created an average kid? My God, how terrible.

Their son was a delightful, well-adjusted, average-IQ person. I told the parents that there was nothing wrong with their son. That he was, in fact, a pretty well put together person. I went on to say that in his social adjustments he was above average. He had many good friends and he related well. He was also a happy child.

"But why is he making C's?" they asked. "He's always made at least B's."

"For one thing he's got other interests," I said.

"For another, the private school he's in now is tougher than the public school you had him in last year."

Our conversation was going rather well until I added, "What's wrong with C's?"

They were appalled. They left. They found another psychologist. Sometimes I think Tom Sawyer recruited help for the fence because he knew how Aunt Polly's critical eye loved perfection—and he didn't want to take the rap by himself.

Being average means making peace with ambivalence. It means that I am good in some things and bad in others and that's as it should be. It means admitting I have areas in which I am very smart and areas in which I am stupid and knowing I don't have to make my smart, perfection and my stupid, inferiority. How trite to say none of us are perfect. But how smugly egotistical to add, But we must try to be. To be average means to swing between "with it" and "out of it"; compassion and not caring; patience and impatience; tolerance and prejudice; love and hate. Average says no to the rhyme, When I am good I am very, very good and when I am bad I am horrid. That's the old superior-inferior swing. Average says, instead, When I am good I really am pretty good—not perfect, just fairly good; and when I am bad I am not *that* bad—except sometimes.

Grace says, I accept you now and you don't even have to sign up for a self-improvement course. Grace also says, Quit bragging about your inferiority, and adds, I've taken care of that.

When Paul talks about "the good I would," he's admitting he's not able to pull off the superior, perfect life. He confesses he failed his Pharisee exam, and if anyone might have passed, it would have been Paul. But inferiority? He rejects that by his very strutty stance, bold preaching, and by taking on all comers with equality. He looks neither up to people nor down, just eye to eye, straight across. He knows who he is.

People often say to me apologetically, "I'm not really good at anything." But who is? Who do you know who's an absolute authority on anything? Furthermore, why would you want to be? Why can't you like yourself just being average like the rest of us folks, fairly good at some things and fairly bad at others? What a relief!